I AM UNIQUE

MARLA CONN

Rourke
Educational Media

A Division of
Carson
Dellosa
Education

Photo Glossary

 **clothing**

 **dancing**

 **family**

 **fingerprint**

 **hair**

 **writing**

High Frequency Words:
- is
- my
- unique

My **hair** is unique.

hair

My **family** is unique.

7

My **writing** is unique.

8

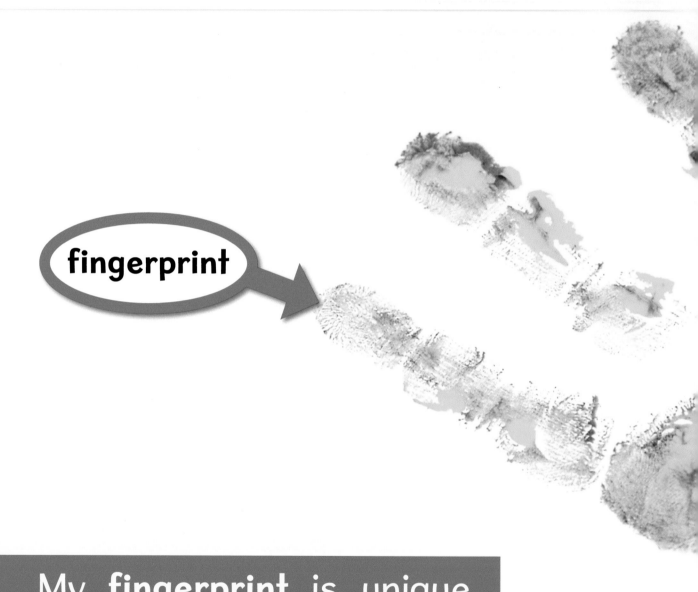

fingerprint

My **fingerprint** is unique.

My **clothing** is unique.

clothing

My **dancing** is unique.

dancing

Activity

1. On the board, write: **Everyone is special.** Discuss with the group.

2. Have students read the story again with a partner. Discuss how each child shown is unique.

3. As a class, think of other words that mean "unique." Include these words and phrases: **special**, **different**, **individual**, **uncommon**, **one and only**.

4. Ask: Which one of the children in the story do you relate to best? How are you unique?

5. Follow these directions to play a game with the group:
   - Write each child's name on a slip of paper. Put all of the names in a box.
   - Have each child pull out a name.
   - Think of something special about that person. How are they unique?
   - Share with the group.